## 21st
## Century
## Skills Library

REAL WORLD MATH: GEOGRAPHY

# GLACIERS

BY BARBARA A. SOMERVILL

CHERRY
LAKE
Publishing

Published in the United States of America by
Cherry Lake Publishing, Ann Arbor, Michigan
www.cherrylakepublishing.com

**Content Adviser**
Andrew Dombard, Associate Professor, Department of Earth and Environmental
Sciences, University of Illinois at Chicago
Math Adviser: Tonya Walker, MA, Boston University

**Credits**
Photos: Cover and page 1, ©David Thyberg, used under license from Shutterstock, Inc.;
page 4, ©iStockphoto.com/NNehring; page 7, ©Charlydamart/Dreamstime.com;
page 8, ©Aero17/Dreamstime.com; pages 10 and 22, ©Jan Martin Will, used
under license from Shutterstock, Inc.; page 12, ©Armin Rose, used under license
from Shutterstock, Inc.; page 14, ©Bridgetjones/Dreamstime.com; page 16,
©hektoR, used under license from Shutterstock, Inc.; page 19, ©Ulrich Doering/
Alamy; page 20, ©Gaja/Dreamstime.com; page 24, ©Svetlana Privezentseva, used
under license from Shutterstock, Inc.; page 27, ©Ron Niebrugge/Alamy

**Library of Congress Cataloging-in-Publication Data**
Somervill, Barbara A.
  Glaciers / by Barbara A. Somervill.
    p. cm.—(Real world math: geography)
  Includes index.
  ISBN-13: 978-1-60279-495-5
  ISBN-10: 1-60279-495-2
  1. Glaciers—Juvenile literature. I. Title. II. Series.
  GB2403.S65 2010
  551.31'2—dc22                    2008047265

Cherry Lake Publishing would like to acknowledge
the work of The Partnership for 21st Century Skills.
Please visit *www.21stcenturyskills.org* for more information.

# TABLE OF CONTENTS

CHAPTER ONE
# WHAT IS A GLACIER?

Glacial ice covers mountain peaks and fills mountain valleys. It spreads over plains and reaches to the sea. Glaciers can cover an area as small as a football field or as large as a continent.

*Receding glaciers in Alaska carved out Glacier Bay. The bay first appeared in the 1700s. Today, it's about 65 miles long.*

A glacier is a mass of ice that begins as snow. A glacier builds when more snow falls than melts over a long period of time. This does not happen quickly. Glacier ice collects over hundreds, even thousands, of years. The ice at the base of some Canadian Arctic ice caps is more than 100,000 years old. Every continent except Australia has glaciers. Glaciers in Africa, however, are rare.

The longest glacier in North America is the Bering Glacier. It measures 118 miles (190 kilometers) long. The largest glacier mass is found in Antarctica. That continent's ice sheet covers about 5 million square miles (13 million sq km) of land. Antarctic ice is thick and heavy. In the western region, ice has pushed the land down to about 1.6 miles (2.6 km) below sea level.

Glacial ice can change the profile of land. Within the ice, glaciers carry tons of soil, rock, and plant matter. Like nature's bulldozer, glaciers flatten mountains. They also carve out deep valleys, such as Yosemite Valley in California. Glaciers carve out land like giant ice cream scoops. The holes left behind may become lakes. That is how the Great Lakes were formed.

There are many types of glaciers. Two types include continental glaciers and **alpine** glaciers. Continental glaciers are broad regions of ice that cover a large area. They flow over mountains, cliffs, and valleys. These very large ice sheets spread out from a central area. They are somewhat dome-shaped. They cover more than 19,300 square miles (49,987 sq km). They are only found in Antarctica and Greenland.

Alpine glaciers are found in mountain regions. Valley glaciers are a type of alpine glacier. They flow down into valley regions. Glaciers in the Andes, Himalayas, and Rocky Mountains are alpine or valley glaciers. Sometimes an alpine glacier flows out of a valley and spreads across a flat plain. This forms a new glacier, called a **piedmont** glacier. Alaska's Malaspina Glacier is a piedmont glacier.

## 21ST CENTURY CONTENT

A severe shortage of water is a serious issue in many parts of the world. Glaciers and ice caps cover nearly 10 percent of Earth's land. They also contain about 70 percent of Earth's freshwater. An iceberg is a large chunk of floating ice that has broken off from a glacier. Some people have suggested collecting icebergs and towing them to areas hit by **drought**. The icebergs, once melted, could provide people in those areas with water.

Do you think this is a good emergency solution? What challenges might prevent this idea from succeeding?

*Glaciers from the Andes, such as the Perito Moreno, flow down through Chile and Argentina.*

Some valley glaciers reach as far as the sea. These are called **tidewater** glaciers. They produce icebergs. Several tidewater glaciers **calve** icebergs in Glacier Bay, Alaska. Calving is the process in which large sections of ice break off a glacier or ice shelf. These detached ice chunks—now called icebergs—drop into the ocean. Every iceberg produced during the process is different.

*Calving can be a huge event. The glacier's edge cracks off and tumbles into the water. The sound of the cracking can be heard for miles.*

# REAL WORLD MATH CHALLENGE

Read the chart. Then use a calculator to answer the questions below.

**Estimate of Global Water Distribution**

| Water Source | Water Volume, in cubic kilometers | Percent of Total Water | Percent of Total Freshwater |
|---|---|---|---|
| Ice caps, glaciers, and permanent snow | 24,064,000 | ? | ? |
| Total global freshwater | 35,030,000 | 2.5% | 100% |
| Total global water (salt water and freshwater) | 1,386,000,000 | 100% | |

**What percentage of total global water is held in ice caps, glaciers, and permanent snow? What percentage of total global freshwater is held in ice caps, glaciers, and permanent snow?**

*(Turn to page 29 for the answers)*

CHAPTER TWO
# THE ANTARCTIC ICE SHEET

What was the weather like 300,000 years ago? How much snow fell during the last ice age? Scientists search for the answers to these questions and many more in Antarctica's ice sheet. They drill deep into the ice to get

*Scientists sometimes use helicopters to travel when they work in Antarctica.*

samples. They read the samples much like you might read a time line in a history book. The glacier's ice recorded droughts, periods of **global warming**, ice ages, and dust storms. Some samples hold bits of ash from massive volcanic eruptions. They even have tiny pieces of pollen from faraway lands.

## LEARNING & INNOVATION SKILLS

Scientists would not be able to answer many questions about Antarctica without the help of technology. For example, NASA **satellites** gather information about the continent. This data helps produce maps showing surface features that have never been seen before. The maps also show which direction the ice is flowing.

Scientists also use technology in creative ways. Attaching special monitoring devices to certain seals has helped experts make interesting discoveries. The waters around Antarctica are becoming less salty. This is probably caused by melting ice. High-tech tools will continue to help solve the mystery of how melting glacial ice affects the planet.

Scientists hope that the ice time line will give us clues to what may happen in the future. They see patterns of global warming in Antarctic ice. They think that current trends in global warming are being written in the ice today.

Scientists have found that Antarctic ice shelves are losing ice more quickly than they would like. Ice shelves are floating branches of the ice sheet. Ice shelves in the West Antarctic Peninsula have been falling apart faster than glacial ice on the rest of Antarctica. Between 1992 and 2006, the western region lost approximately 100 billion tons of ice per year. The eastern region lost almost no ice at all.

*This image shows large cracks in Larsen B which was one of three parts of the Larsen Ice Shelf. Larsen A and B are both gone. Larsen C is still there.*

During the past 50 years, Antarctica has lost several ice shelves completely. They include Prince Gustav Channel, Larsen Inlet, Larsen B, Wordie, Muller, and the Jones Ice Shelf. The Ross and Wilkins ice shelves have calved huge icebergs. The high rate of ice loss suggests that global warming's effect on the region is increasing.

Why is this important? Water does not disappear from Earth. It just changes form. Glacier ice melts and adds water to the oceans. Worldwide, sea level is approximately 6 to 8 inches (15 to 20 centimeters) higher than it was 100 years ago. This increase results from warmer seawater and melting glaciers. If too much ice melts, sea level will increase even more.

## REAL WORLD MATH CHALLENGE

The world's largest iceberg broke off the Ross Ice Shelf in March 2000. The iceberg was named B-15. Its overall area was 11,000 square kilometers. B-15 did not go far. It got caught in the sea ice. In 2002 and 2003, B-15 broke into smaller pieces. One broken piece named B-15A became the largest free-floating object in the world. B-15A measured approximately 122 kilometers long and 27 kilometers wide. **What was the area of B-15A?**

(Turn to page 29 for the answer)

CHAPTER THREE

# DO THE MATH: GLACIERS ON THE MOVE

Antarctic glaciers are not the only glaciers that are changing. Glaciers worldwide are on the move. Some are advancing. Most, however, are retreating.

*Scientists think the Monaco Glacier in Spitsbergen, Svalbard, moved about 1.2 miles (2 kilometers) in 6 years.*

Some glaciers move in odd ways. A **surge** glacier can rush forward at a rate that is up to 100 times faster than normal. No one knows exactly why glaciers race forward. The rush, however, only lasts a short time. Glaciers in Svalbard (an island group that makes up the northernmost part of Norway), the Canadian Arctic, Alaska, and Antarctica are currently surging forward.

 **LIFE & CAREER SKILLS**

International **Polar** Year (IPY) was a large scientific program. It ran for two years, from March 2007 to March 2009. Scientists did research in harsh polar environments. They studied the Arctic and Antarctic regions. They looked into every aspect of polar life. They also studied changes in sea ice.

The success of IPY depended on the **collective** efforts of many experts. Thousands of people from more than 60 countries were involved in the research. Together, these scientists studied how changes in the regions might affect the rest of the world.

In Antarctica, three huge glaciers have sped up in the last 10 years. The glacier that causes the most worry is the Pine Island Glacier. This glacier is around 1.2 miles (2 km) thick and 18.6 miles (30 km) wide. Pine Island Glacier is moving forward at a speedy 2.2 miles (3.5 km) per year. When the glacier reaches the ocean, it calves icebergs.

Greenland's Kangerdlugssuaq Glacier flows forward 8.7 miles (14 km) per year. Scientists carefully measure this ice

*Crevasses can make walking on glacial ice very dangerous.*

sheet. They know that it is losing ice at a frightening pace. Ice loss has more than doubled in 10 years. It has increased from a loss of 21.6 cubic miles (90 cubic km) per year to a loss of 53.7 cubic miles (224 cubic km) per year. That is a lot of ice.

When glaciers move, changes appear on the surface of the ice. The ice cracks. Deep **crevasses** form. In some cases, the shifting ice produces sharp, jagged **pinnacles**.

While some glaciers charge ahead, others retreat. Mountain glaciers around the world are in a stage of retreat. They are melting.

In the high Andes of Peru, Pastoruri Glacier has retreated 656 feet (200 meters) in 10 years. Overall, Peru has lost more than 20 percent of its glaciers in the past 30 years. Some Peruvians depend on glacial meltwater to survive. If the glaciers disappear, there will be no water for drinking or for crops.

## REAL WORLD MATH CHALLENGE

In 1953, the Kutiah Glacier in Pakistan surged forward 12 kilometers in 107 days. **In meters, what is the average distance the glacier surged each day?** (Hint: Remember that there are 1,000 meters in 1 kilometer.) Round your answer to the nearest whole number.

(Turn to page 29 for the answer)

Glaciers help scientists understand climate change. Scientists look for climate trends over a long period of time. By studying different types of glaciers, they can gather different information. For example, temperature and precipitation changes can be measured easily in small, contained mountain glaciers.

## REAL WORLD MATH CHALLENGE

The Muir tidewater glacier has been observed for nearly 200 years. During the nine-year period from 1941 to 1950, the glacier receded approximately 3,000 meters. From 1976 to 1978, the glacier also receded approximately 3,000 meters. During the past 200 years, Muir Glacier has receded at an average rate of 450 meters per year. **How many meters per year did Muir Glacier retreat between 1941 and 1950? Did the ice recede faster during that period or from 1976 to 1978? How many meters has the glacier retreated in the past 200 years?** Round your answers to the nearest whole number.

*(Turn to page 29 for the answers)*

*Mt. Kilimanjaro is quickly losing its glaciers. Scientists are trying to learn as much as they can before the glaciers disappear.*

CHAPTER FOUR

# DO THE MATH: CALVING ICEBERGS

Seeing a glacier calve an iceberg is amazing. The process produces an ear-piercing sound. The result? A massive ice cube that floats along with ocean currents.

Most icebergs calve off Greenland's glaciers and Antarctica's ice sheets. Approximately 40,000 medium to

*An iceberg floats off the coast of Greenland. Icebergs in this part of the world usually last about 3 years.*

large icebergs calve every year in Greenland. Antarctica produces fewer icebergs, but they are much larger.

## LEARNING & INNOVATION SKILLS

In 1912, the *Titanic* ocean liner hit an iceberg in the North Atlantic Ocean and sank. Today, we rarely hear about ships sinking due to collisions with icebergs. Why? Icebergs are monitored. Special satellites are one tool used to track the movement of dangerous icebergs.

Satellite radar detects ships, oil platforms, sea ice, and icebergs. The radar signal returned from icebergs is different than the signals coming from objects such as ships. Experts carefully review these radar images and data. Is the ship approaching sea ice? A small island? An iceberg? Knowing how to analyze and interpret this information is important. It helps keep ships safe.

There are six size categories of icebergs. The smallest ones are called growlers. They are around the size of a car. Bergy bits are larger—the size of a small house. The last four sizes are small, medium, large, and very large icebergs. A true iceberg rises at least 16.4 feet (5 m) above the water's surface.

It must also measure at least 49.2 feet (15 m) wide at the water line. Very large icebergs rise more than 246.1 feet (75 m) above the sea. They are more than 698.8 feet (213 m) wide. In Antarctica, an iceberg named B-15 broke off the Ross Ice Shelf. This iceberg covered an area about the size of Connecticut.

Shape, size, air pockets, and other factors affect how an iceberg floats. Roughly 80 to 90 percent of an iceberg is under water. That is where the danger lies. In the past, hundreds of ships have sunk after striking the underwater part of an iceberg.

These floating ice islands may reflect shades of blue, green, and white against the brilliant sunlight. Their shapes vary.

*Icebergs are dangerous because so much of an iceberg is under water and cannot be seen.*

Some are flat masses. Others are towering peaks. Some look like icy pyramids. The official shapes include **tabular** icebergs, which have flat tops. Domed versions are rounded. Wedge varieties are shaped like pyramids. Pinnacle versions have tall peaks. **Drydock icebergs** have a sunken area in the center.

An iceberg may have large air bubbles. As the iceberg melts, the bubbles appear on the surface. These icebergs take on strange shapes.

Icebergs begin to melt as soon as they break away from the glacier. Ocean currents carry icebergs. All polar currents head toward the equator. The iceberg slowly melts away as it reaches warmer waters. Its water becomes part of the ocean. By the time an iceberg reaches 40 degrees latitude, it has usually melted. Icebergs may take several years to completely disappear.

## REAL WORLD MATH CHALLENGE

An iceberg calves off the Pine Island Glacier in Antarctica. Only 10% of the iceberg is above water. That means 90% of the iceberg is below water. The total volume of the iceberg is 1,630,000 cubic meters. **What is the volume of the section of iceberg that is above water? What is the volume of the section of iceberg that is below water?** You may want to use a calculator.

*(Turn to page 29 for the answers)*

CHAPTER FIVE
# GLOBAL WARMING

Imagine a world that looks very different from the one that exists now. That's what many scientists fear as the world's glaciers continue to melt. Sea level rises as melting ice seeps into the oceans. In the future, many of the areas we now

*The Briksdalsbreen Glacier in Norway keeps shrinking. Scientists say it is the smallest it has been since the year 1200.*

consider coasts—and the cities near them—could be under water. Many experts point to climate change and the rising temperatures of global warming as the reason why Earth's glaciers are shrinking.

For many years, scientists have tried to measure changes in the size of glaciers. Teams drilled holes in the ice in order to take measurements. They placed measuring sticks into the holes. They carefully recorded changes in the glacier's surface level over time. Using this method, scientists measured changes in approximately 350 glaciers. But the process was expensive. It required people to visit every stick regularly in order to record any changes.

Today, satellites and planes allow scientists to learn more about glaciers. Laser technology is used to measure changes in a glacier's surface. Scientists are able to measure changes in thousands of glaciers every year with the help of lasers.

Glacier ice around the world is melting. And it has melted at a faster rate in the past 25 years than it has for several hundred years. Even ancient glaciers that survived for hundreds of thousands of years are disappearing. Africa's major glaciers are found on Mount Kilimanjaro in Tanzania. These glaciers have lost 82 percent of their ice since 1912. By 2020, Kilimanjaro's glaciers may disappear completely.

Ice loss is also occurring in Europe's Alps mountain range and New Zealand's mountains. Greenland and Antarctic ice sheets lose ice daily, too.

## REAL WORLD MATH CHALLENGE

The World Glacier Monitoring Service worked with the United Nations Environment Programme to study glaciers. Experts measured 30 major glaciers from 1980 to 2001. Read the graph below. Then answer the questions that follow.

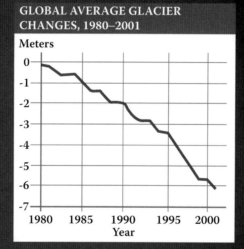

GLOBAL AVERAGE GLACIER CHANGES, 1980–2001

In meters, what was the total ice loss of the glaciers studied from 1980 to 1990? Was the loss of ice greater from 1980 to 1985 or from 1995 to 2000? What was the total loss for all glaciers from 1980 to 2000?

Note: Assume that the ice loss totaled 3.4 meters in 1995 and 5.6 meters in 2000.

[Turn to page 29 for the answers]

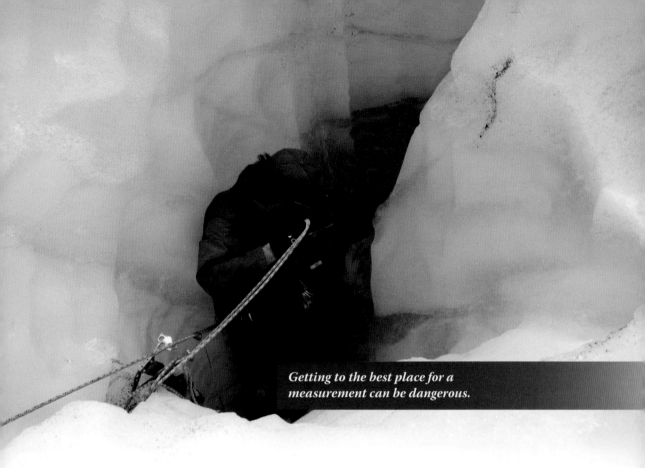

*Getting to the best place for a measurement can be dangerous.*

Scientists unlock the history of our planet in glacial ice. They also try to predict the planet's future by watching the loss of that same ice. They hope that plans to slow the rate of global warming may also slow ice loss. Some estimate that if all the glaciers and ice sheets melted, sea level could rise by as much as 328 feet (100 m). What does that mean? All coastal cities would be under water. Many islands would disappear beneath the seas.

## 21ˢᵀ CENTURY CONTENT

The Intergovernmental Panel on Climate Change (IPCC) was established in 1988. Climate change is complex. It doesn't just affect one nation. It affects people, wildlife, and agriculture around the world. That is partly why the organization is made up of members from government and scientific groups from many different countries.

The IPCC was created to evaluate the latest information on climate change. This information includes possible causes of climate change and its effects on the economy or environment. Data also includes ways to cope with these challenges. This information is useful when government leaders and lawmakers work to decide what to do about climate change.

These effects may not happen right away. But changes in the world's glaciers shout a loud warning: the ice is melting.

# REAL WORLD MATH
# CHALLENGE ANSWERS

## Chapter One

Page 9
The percentage of total global water held in ice caps, glaciers, and permanent snow is 1.7%.
24,064,000 ÷ 1,386,000,000 = 0.017 = 1.7%
The percentage of total global freshwater held in ice caps, glaciers, and permanent snow is 68.7%.
24,064,000 ÷ 35,030,000 = 0.687 = 68.7%

## Chapter Two

Page 13
B-15A had an area of 3,294 square kilometers.
122 km x 27 km = 3,294 sq km

## Chapter Three

Page 17
The Kutiah Glacier in Pakistan surged forward an average of 112 meters per day.
12 km ÷ 107 days = 0.1121 km/day
0.1121 x 1,000 m = 112.1 = 112 m/day

Page 18
Muir Glacier retreated 333 meters per year between 1941 and 1950.
3,000 m ÷ 9 years = 333.3 = 333 m/year
The ice receded faster between 1976 and 1978 than between 1941 and 1950.
3,000 m ÷ 2 years = 1,500 m/year
The glacier retreated 90,000 meters during the past 200 years.
450 m x 200 years = 90,000 m

## Chapter Four

Page 23
The volume of the section of iceberg that is above water is 163,000 cubic meters.
10% = 0.10
1,630,000 cubic m x 0.10 = 163,000 cubic m
The volume of the section of iceberg that is below water is 1,467,000 cubic meters.
90% = 0.90
1,630,000 cubic m x 0.90 = 1,467,000 cubic m

## Chapter Five

Page 26
The total ice loss of the glaciers studied from 1980 to 1990 was 2 meters.
1980 = 0 meters
1990 = –2 meters
–2 m – 0 m = –2 m (a loss of 2 meters)

The loss of ice was greater from 1995 to 2000.
1980 = 0 m
1985 = –1 m
–1 m – 0 m = –1 m (a loss of 1 meter)
1995 = –3.4 m
2000 = –5.6 m
–5.6 m – –3.4 m = –5.6 m + 3.4 m = –2.2 m (a loss of 2.2 meters)

The total loss for all glaciers from 1980 to 2000 was 5.6 meters.
2000 = –5.6 m
1980 = 0 m
–5.6 m – 0 m = –5.6 m (a loss of 5.6 meters)

# GLOSSARY

**alpine (AL-pine)** having to do with mountains

**calve (KAV)** to separate or break away; icebergs are formed when large chunks of ice break away from an ice mass

**collective (kuh-LEK-tiv)** having to do with a group of people or things

**crevasses (kruh-VASS-iz)** deep cracks in glacial ice

**drought (DROUT)** a long period of very little or no rain

**drydock icebergs (DRYE-dok EYESS-bergz)** icebergs that have a sunken area near the center that reaches into, or comes close to, the waterline

**global warming (GLOH-buhl WOR-meeng)** an overall rise in world temperatures

**piedmont (PEED-mont)** near or formed at the base of mountains

**pinnacles (PIN-uh-kuhlz)** tall peaks

**polar (POH-lur)** having to do with the areas around the North Pole or South Pole

**satellites (SAT-uh-lites)** spacecraft that orbit Earth

**surge (SURJ)** a rush forward

**tabular (TAB-yuh-lur)** having a flat surface

**tidewater (TIDE-waw-tur)** low-lying coastal land

# FOR MORE INFORMATION

## BOOKS

Green, Robert. *Global Warming.* Ann Arbor, MI: Cherry Lake Publishing, 2008.

Sepehri, Sandy. *Glaciers.* Vero Beach, FL: Rourke Publishing, 2008.

Walker, Sally M. *Glaciers.* Minneapolis: Lerner, 2008.

## WEB SITES

### National Snow and Ice Data Center—All About Glaciers
*nsidc.org/glaciers/quickfacts.html*
Find interesting facts about glaciers

### USGS—Glaciers and Icecaps: Storehouses of Freshwater
*ga.water.usgs.gov/edu/earthglacier.html*
Learn more about glaciers and how they can affect landscapes

### World View of Global Warming—Glaciers and Glacial Warming, Receding Glaciers
*www.worldviewofglobalwarming.org/pages/glaciers.html*
For photos and information about how climate change affects the world's glaciers

# INDEX

## ABOUT THE AUTHOR

**Barbara Somervill** loves to write about science and geography. The Real World Math series provided her with the opportunity to combine interesting facts with practical applications. Barbara has written nearly 200 children's books and school textbooks. Every book is an opportunity to learn about new and different subjects. She is married, a mother, and a grandmother, and she lives in South Carolina.